Plato: Shaping the Philosophy of Western Thought

Plato, one of the most influential philosophers in Western history, was born in Athens, Greece, around 428/427 BC. His birth name was Aristocles, but he later acquired the nickname "Plato," meaning "broad" or "wide," possibly a reference to his robust physique or the breadth of his philosophical ideas.

Plato hailed from a prominent and aristocratic family. His father, Ariston, was believed to be descended from the legendary Athenian king Codrus, and his mother, Perictione, was related to the great Athenian statesman Solon. It is said that even in his early years, Plato showed an inclination for intellectual pursuits and was a gifted student. His family's social status and wealth ensured that he received the best education Athens had to offer.

As a young man, Plato became acquainted with the works of the renowned philosopher Socrates, who had a profound impact on his life and philosophical development. Socrates' method of dialectical questioning and pursuit of truth greatly influenced Plato and laid the foundation for his own philosophical inquiries.

During his youth, Athens was a hub of intellectual and political activity. It was the birthplace of democracy and a center for philosophical discourse. Plato witnessed the city's transformation during a turbulent period, which included the Peloponnesian War between Athens and Sparta, as well as the execution of his mentor, Socrates, in 399 BC, on charges of impiety and corrupting the youth.

Following Socrates' death, Plato left Athens and embarked on a series of travels, visiting Egypt, where he likely studied geometry and mathematics, and the Greek city of Cyrene, among other places. He may have also spent time in southern Italy and Sicily, coming into contact with various philosophical traditions and political systems.

These experiences played a pivotal role in shaping Plato's philosophical outlook and his views on the ideal society. He became convinced that Athenian democracy was flawed and prone to tyranny, and he began to develop his own theories about governance, justice, and the nature of reality.

Major Works by Plato

Plato's writings, particularly his dialogues, are the bedrock of Western philosophy, addressing a wide spectrum of fundamental questions and philosophical themes. In these dialogues, he navigates through the complexities of human existence, governance, and the nature of reality.

"The Republic", undoubtedly one of his most significant works, stands as a crowning achievement. In this dialogue, Plato explores the nature of justice and presents a vision of the ideal state, governed by philosopher-kings. The "Allegory of the Cave," embedded within "The Republic," symbolizes the journey from ignorance to wisdom, exemplifying Plato's skill in allegorical storytelling.

In "The Symposium," Plato delves into the intricate nature of love and desire, offering diverse perspectives on the subject through a series of speeches by different characters, including Socrates.

"The Phaedo" delves into profound questions concerning the immortality of the soul. In the context of recounting Socrates' final moments, it presents his philosophical reflections on death and the afterlife.

"The Gorgias" takes on the issues of rhetoric and its connection to justice, while "The Meno" raises questions about the teachability of virtue and introduces the intriguing concept of "anamnesis," or the recollection of knowledge.

Plato's cosmological speculations come to the forefront in "The Timaeus," where he presents a theory on the creation of the universe and the nature of the physical world.

In his final and longest work, "The Laws," Plato envisions an ideal society and examines the role of law in shaping human behavior, extending his exploration of justice and ethics.

Later Life and Legacy

In the latter part of his life, Plato continued to refine his philosophical ideas and played a pivotal role in establishing and overseeing the Academy, a groundbreaking institution that would become a hub for intellectual discourse in Athens. The Academy, founded around 387 BC, was situated in a grove dedicated to the hero Academus, located just outside the city's walls.

This institution was a unique center for philosophical, mathematical, and scientific research and education, which differed from conventional educational structures of the time.

At the Academy, Plato passionately nurtured an environment where philosophical discussions, debates, and the pursuit of knowledge thrived. It was not merely a school but a gathering place for philosophers, students, and scholars to come together and engage in intellectual exploration. Lectures, dialogues, and dialectical reasoning were the order of the day, designed to stimulate critical thinking and encourage the pursuit of wisdom.

Plato, serving as the head of the Academy, took it upon himself to impart his philosophical ideas and methods to his students. Among the many notable individuals who benefited from Plato's tutelage was Aristotle, who would later go on to establish his own school, the Lyceum, and become one of the most influential philosophers in history.

Plato's intellectual pursuits did not hinder his involvement in politics. He actively maintained connections with various rulers and governments in Syracuse, Sicily, as part of his effort to implement his political ideals. Regrettably, these endeavors yielded limited success and even posed danger to him. His experiences in Syracuse, chronicled in his letters, serve as a cautionary tale about the challenges of translating philosophical ideals into practical politics.

Upon his death around 348/347 BC, Plato left behind a rich intellectual legacy. His dialogues and writings have been studied, interpreted, and debated for centuries. His students and successors, most notably Aristotle, carried forward and expanded upon his ideas, influencing the development of Western thought in profound ways.

The Academy, established by Plato, remained active for several centuries, contributing to the growth of Hellenistic and Roman philosophy. Its profound impact on education and philosophical inquiry is a testament to Plato's enduring influence.

Plato's ideas have transcended time and culture, shaping the course of Western philosophy and leaving an indelible mark on subjects ranging from ethics and politics to metaphysics and epistemology. His work continues to be a source of inspiration and debate for scholars, philosophers, and thinkers in the modern era.

Major Ideas and Philosophy of Plato

Plato's life and work were profoundly shaped by the intellectual and political environment of ancient Athens. His contributions to philosophy offer enduring insights into the nature of reality, knowledge, and the human condition.

1. THE THEORY OF FORMS (THEORY OF IDEAS): Perhaps Plato's most enduring and influential concept, the Theory of Forms, posits the existence of a non-material realm of perfect, eternal Forms or Ideas.

These Forms represent the true reality and are the objects of knowledge, while the physical world is an imperfect copy. This theory had a profound impact on metaphysics and epistemology and continues to be a topic of philosophical debate.

2. DIALOGUES: Plato's philosophical ideas are primarily conveyed through a series of dialogues, which are written in the form of conversations between his mentor, Socrates, and other prominent figures of his time. These dialogues serve as both a medium for philosophical inquiry and a vehicle for exploring and presenting his ideas. Some of his most famous dialogues include "The Symposium," which discusses the nature of love, and "The Republic," where he explores the ideal state. These dialogues not only offer insights into his philosophical system but also showcase his commitment to the Socratic method of inquiry and the pursuit of truth through reasoned discourse. They remain essential texts in the history of philosophy and provide a foundation for much of Western thought.

3. THE REPUBLIC: "The Republic" is one of Plato's most significant works and a cornerstone of political philosophy and ethics. In this dialogue, Plato articulates his vision of the ideal state, one governed by philosopher-kings who possess both wisdom and a deep understanding of justice. The work delves into the nature of justice, the philosopher's role in society, and the importance of education in forming virtuous citizens.

It also explores the allegory of the just city as an allegory for the just soul, connecting the microcosm of the individual to the macrocosm of the state. "The Republic" continues to stimulate discussions about the nature of justice and the structure of the ideal society.

4. THE ALLEGORY OF THE CAVE: Plato's famous allegory is found within "The Republic" and serves as a powerful metaphor for his views on education and enlightenment. In this allegory, he describes prisoners who are chained in a dark cave, their only perception of reality being the shadows of objects cast on the cave wall by a fire behind them. The prisoners believe these shadows are the true objects, representing their limited and false perception of reality. The escape from the cave and the journey to the outside world symbolize the process of philosophical enlightenment and the shift from ignorance to wisdom. This allegory underscores the transformative power of education and the philosopher's role in leading individuals toward the truth.

5. EPISTEMOLOGY: Plato's exploration of epistemology, the study of knowledge, challenged prevailing ideas of his time. He argued that true knowledge is not derived solely from sensory experience but is innate and can be recalled through dialectical reasoning. His concept of anamnesis, or the recollection of knowledge, is exemplified in the dialogue "Meno." In this dialogue, Socrates leads a slave boy to "remember" a geometric theorem through a series of questions, suggesting that knowledge is already present in the soul and merely needs to be awakened.

Plato's epistemological ideas have had a profound influence on the development of rationalism, a philosophical tradition that emphasizes the role of reason and innate ideas in the acquisition of knowledge.

6. IDEAL STATE AND POLITICS: In "The Republic," Plato offers a detailed vision of an ideal state. He believes that the just city should be structured hierarchically, with different classes of citizens: rulers, guardians, and producers. The rulers, or philosopher-kings, are those with the highest wisdom and virtue, and they are best suited to govern. Guardians are responsible for the defense of the state, while producers engage in economic activities. This hierarchical structure reflects Plato's conviction that individuals should fulfill roles according to their innate abilities and aptitudes. The work also explores the nature of justice, with Plato arguing that true justice is the harmony of the individual and the state, and it underscores the pivotal role of education in shaping virtuous citizens.

7. SOCRATIC METHOD: Building on the methodology of his mentor Socrates, Plato extensively employs the Socratic method in his dialogues. This method involves a series of questions and answers aimed at uncovering truth and gaining a deeper understanding of complex concepts. It encourages critical thinking and self-examination. Through this dialectical questioning, Plato explores fundamental questions about ethics, morality, and the nature of reality, thereby advancing the pursuit of knowledge and wisdom.

8. ETHICS AND VIRTUE: Plato contends that the highest good is the ultimate fulfillment of the human soul. For Plato, the cardinal virtues include wisdom, temperance, courage, and justice. He believes that these virtues are interconnected, and living a life in accordance with them leads to true happiness and moral uprightness. This ethical framework influenced the development of virtue ethics, a major tradition in moral philosophy.

9. DUALISM: Plato's distinction between the world of the physical and the world of the Forms has profound implications for metaphysics and epistemology. He believed that the soul is immortal and preexists its incarnation in the material world. This dualism between the eternal, unchanging realm of the Forms and the ever-changing world of the physical laid the foundation for later philosophical concepts such as mind-body dualism, notably explored by René Descartes. Plato's ideas on the immortality of the soul and its preexistence have had a lasting impact on philosophical discussions concerning the nature of the self and the afterlife.

10. ART AND AESTHETICS: In "The Republic," Plato expresses reservations about the influence of art on the soul and its capacity to educate. He believed that art, including poetry and literature, had the potential to shape individual and societal values. Consequently, he argued that art should be closely regulated and censored if it didn't align with the standards of the ideal city. His views on art and aesthetics reflect his broader concerns about the impact of culture and the arts on morality and the formation of a just society.

They assembled together and dedicated these as the first-fruits of their love to Apollo in his Delphic temple, inscribing there those maxims which are on every tongue—'know thyself' and 'Nothing overmuch.'

The productions of
all arts are kinds
of poetry and
their craftsmen
are all poets.

The first step in learning is the destruction of human conceit.

Beauty of style and harmony and grace and good rhythm depend on Simplicity.

Bodily exercise, when
compulsory, does no
harm to the body;
but knowledge which
is acquired under
compulsion obtains
no hold on the mind.

He who is of a calm
and happy nature
will hardly feel the
pressure of age, but
to him who is of an
opposite disposition
youth and age are
equally a burden.

Grant that I may become beautiful in my soul within, and that all my external possessions may be in harmony with my inner self. May I consider the wise to be rich, and may I have such riches as only a person of self-restraint can bear or endure.

In every man there is
an eye of the soul,
which...is more
precious far than
ten thousand bodily
eyes, for by it alone
is truth seen.

According to Greek mythology, humans were originally created with four arms, four legs and a head with two faces. Fearing their power, Zeus split them into two separate parts, condemning them to spend their lives in search of their other halves.

Until philosophers are kings, or the kings and princes of this world have the spirit and power of philosophy, and political greatness and wisdom meet in one, and those commoner natures who pursue either to the exclusion of the other are compelled to stand aside, cities will never have rest from their evils – no, nor the human race, as I believe – and then only will this our State have a possibility of life and behold the light of day.

Let the speaker
speak truly and the
judge decide justly.

The worst of all
deceptions is
self-deception.

And may we not say,
Adeimantus, that the
most gifted minds,
when they are ill-
educated, become
the worst?

When the tyrant has disposed of foreign enemies by conquest or treaty, and there is nothing to fear from them, then he is always stirring up some war or other, in order that the people may require a leader.

Desires are only the
lack of something:
and those who have the
greatest desires are in
a worse condition than
those who have none, or
very slight ones.

...if a man can be properly said to love something, it must be clear that he feels affection for it as a whole, and does not love part of it to the exclusion of the rest.

Since those who rule in the city do so because they own a lot, I suppose they're unwilling to enact laws to prevent young people who've had no discipline from spending and wasting their wealth, so that by making loans to them, secured by the young people's property, and then calling those loans in, they themselves become even richer and more honored.

...when he looks at Beauty in the only way that Beauty can be seen – only then will it become possible for him to give birth not to images of virtue (because he's in touch with no images), but to true virtue [arete] (because he is in touch with true Beauty). The love of the gods belongs to anyone who has given to true virtue and nourished it, and if any human being could become immortal,
it would be he.

If anyone comes to the gates of poetry and expects to become an adequate poet by acquiring expert knowledge of the subject without the Muses' madness, he will fail, and his self-controlled verses will be eclipsed by the poetry of men who have been driven out of their minds.

The lover, who
is true and no
counterfeit, must
of necessity be
loved by his love.

... when someone sees a soul disturbed and unable to see something, he won't laugh mindlessly, but he'll take into consideration whether it has come from a brighter life and is dimmed through not having yet become accustomed to the dark or whether it has come from greater ignorance into greater light and is dazzled by the increased brilliance.

What if the man could
see Beauty Itself, pure,
unalloyed, stripped of
mortality, and all its
pollution, stains, and
vanities, unchanging,
divine,...the man
becoming in that
communion, the friend
of God, himself
immortal;...would that
be a life to disregard?

What a strange thing
that which men call
pleasure seems to be,
and how astonishing
the relation it has
with what is thought to
be its opposite, namely
pain! A man cannot have
both at the same time.
Yet if he pursues and
catches the one, he is
almost always bound to
catch the other also,
like two creatures
with one head.

Those wretches who
never have experienced
the sweets of wisdom
and virtue, but spend
all their time in revels
and debauches, sink
downward day after day,
and make their whole
life one continued
series of errors.

Music and rhythm
find their way
into the secret
places of the soul.

If the head and
the body are to be
well, you must
begin by curing
the soul.

As it is, the lover of inquiry must follow his beloved wherever it may lead him.

It would be better for me ... that multitudes of men should disagree with me rather than that I, being one, should be out of harmony with myself.

Opinion is the
medium between
knowledge and
ignorance.

A life without
investigation is
not worth living.

And Agathon said, It
is probable, Socrates,
that I knew nothing
of what I had said.

And yet spoke you
beautifully, Agathon,
he said.

Then the case is the same in all the other arts for the orator and his rhetoric; there is no need to know the truth of the actual matters, but one merely needs to have discovered some device of persuasion which will make one appear to those who do not know to know better than those who know.

The vicious lover is the follower of earthly Love who desires the body rather than the soul; his heart is set on what is mutable and must therefore be inconstant. And as soon as the body he loves begins to pass the first flower of its beauty, he "spreads his wings and flies away," giving the lie to all his pretty speeches and dishonoring his vows, whereas the lover whose heart is touched by moral beauties is constant all his life, for he has become one with what will never fade.

The philosopher is in love with truth, that is, not with the changing world of sensation, which is the object of opinion, but with the unchanging reality which is the object of knowledge.

Excess generally
causes reaction, and
produces a change in
the opposite direction,
whether it be in the
seasons, or in
individuals, or
in governments.

Of all the things of
a man's soul which
he has within him,
justice is the
greatest good
and injustice
the greatest evil.

How could they see
anything but the
shadows if they
were never allowed
to move their heads?

One of the penalties for refusing to participate in politics is that you end up being governed by your inferiors.

And a democracy, I
suppose, comes into
being when the poor,
winning the victory,
put to death some of the
other party, drive out
others, and grant the
rest of the citizens an
equal share in both
citizenship and
offices.

According to Diotima,
Love is not a god at
all, but is rather a
spirit that mediates
between people and the
objects of their desire.
Love is neither wise
nor beautiful, but is
rather the desire for
wisdom and beauty.

Every dictator
comes up with the
notorious and
typical demand:
he asks the people
for bodyguards to
protect him, the
people's champion.

Democracy, which is
a charming form of
government, full of
variety and disorder,
and dispensing a sort
of equality to equals
and unequals alike.

Nothing beautiful
without struggle.

As the builders say,
the larger stones do
not lie well without
the lesser.

There are three arts
which are concerned
with all things: one
which uses, another
which makes, a third
which imitates them.

No physician, insofar
as he is a physician,
considers his own good
in what he prescribes,
but the good of his
patient; for the true
physician is also a
ruler having the human
body as a subject, and is
not a mere moneymaker.

Have you ever
sensed that our
soul is immortal
and never dies?

The object of
education is to
teach us to love
what is beautiful.

The greatest privilege
of a human life is to
become a midwife to the
awakening of the Soul
in another person.

He whom loves touches
not walks in darkness.

The beginning
is the most important
part of the work.

Not one of them who
took up in his youth
with this opinion
that there are no gods
ever continued until
old age faithful to
his conviction.

Musical innovation is full of danger to the State, for when modes of music change, the fundamental laws of the State always change with them.

There are three
classes of men;
lovers of wisdom,
lovers of honor,
and lovers of gain.

The man who finds that in the course of his life he has done a lot of wrong often wakes up at night in terror, like a child with a nightmare, and his life is full of foreboding: but the man who is conscious of no wrongdoing is filled with cheerfulness and with the comfort of old age.

What shall we say about those spectators, then, who can see a plurality of beautiful things, but not beauty itself, and who are incapable of following if someone else tries to lead them to it, and who can see many moral actions, but not morality itself, and so on? That they only ever entertain beliefs, and do not know any of the things they believe?

If women are
expected to do the
same work as men, we
must teach them the
same things.

Appearance
tyrannizes
over truth.

The power of the Good
has taken refuge in
the nature of the
Beautiful.

And the true order of going, or being led by another, to the things of love, is to begin from the beauties of earth and mount upwards for the sake of that other beauty, using these steps only, and from one going on to two, and from two to all fair forms to fair practices, and from fair practices to fair notions, until from fair notions he arrives at the notion of absolute beauty, and at last knows what the essence of beauty is.

If it were necessary
either to do wrong or
to suffer it, I should
choose to suffer
rather than do it.

What is better adapted
than the festive use
of wine in the first
place to test and in
the second place to
train the character of
a man, if care be taken
in the use of it? What
is there cheaper or
more innocent?

If men learn this, it will implant
forgetfulness in their souls;
they will cease to exercise
memory because they rely on that
which is written, calling things
to remembrance no longer from
within themselves, but by means
of external marks. What you have
discovered is a recipe not for
memory, but for reminder. And it
is no true wisdom that you offer
your disciples, but only its
semblance, for by telling them of
many things without teaching
them you will make them seem to
know much, while for the most
part they know nothing, and as
men filled, not with wisdom, but
with the conceit of wisdom, they
will be a burden to their fellows.

I thought to myself:
I am wiser than this
man; neither of us
probably knows
anything that is
really good, but
he thinks he has
knowledge, when he
has not, while I,
having no knowledge,
do not think I have.

True opinions are a
fine thing and do all
sorts of good so long
as they stay in their
place; but they will
not stay long. They run
away from a man's mind,
so they are not worth
much until you tether
them by working out
the reason. Once they
are tied down, they
become knowledge,
and are stable.

Neither family,
nor privilege, nor
wealth, nor anything
but Love can light
that beacon which a
man must steer by
when he sets out to
live the better life.

Let early
education be a
sort of amusement;
you will then be
better able to
find out the
natural bent.

How can you prove whether at this moment we are sleeping, and all our thoughts are a dream; or whether we are awake, and talking to one another in the waking state?

Great is the issue at
stake, greater than
appears, whether a man
is to be good or bad.
And what will any one
be profited if, under
the influence of money
or power, he neglect
justice and virtue?

For just as poets love their own works, and fathers their own children, in the same way those who have created a fortune value their money, not merely for its uses, like other persons, but because it is their own production. This makes them moreover disagreeable companions, because they will praise nothing but riches.

And first he will see
the shadows best, next
the reflections of men
and other objects in
the water, and then the
objects themselves,
then he will gaze upon
the light of the moon
and the stars and the
spangled heaven...Last
of all he will be able
to see the sun.

...and when one of them meets the other half, the actual half of himself, whether he be a lover of youth or a lover of another sort, the pair are lost in an amazement of love and friendship and intimacy and one will not be out of the other's sight, as I may say, even for a moment...

Education in music
is most sovereign
because more than
anything else rhythm
and harmony find
their way to the
innermost soul and
take strongest
hold upon it.

The love, more
especially, which is
concerned with the good,
and which is perfected
in company with
temperance and justice,
whether among gods or
men, has the greatest
power, and is the source
of all our happiness and
harmony, and makes us
friends with the gods
who are above us, and
with one another.

In those days, when
people were not wise
like you young people,
they were content to
listen to a tree
or a rock in simple
openness, just as long
as it spoke the truth,
but to you, perhaps, it
makes a difference who
is speaking and where
he comes from.

So when the universe was quickened with soul, God was well pleased; and he bethought him to make it yet more like its type. And whereas the type is eternal and nought that is created can be eternal, he devised for it a moving image of abiding eternity, which we call time. And he made days and months and years, which are portions of time; and past and future are forms of time, though we wrongly attribute them also to eternity. For of eternal Being we ought not to say 'it was', 'it shall be', but 'it is' alone: and in like manner we are wrong in saying 'it is' of sensible things which become and perish; for these are ever fleeting and changing, having their existence in time.

Human nature was originally one and we were a whole, and the desire and the pursuit of the whole is called love.

Even if you
can only make a
little progress,
Theaetetus, you
should cheer up.

There should exist
among the citizens
neither extreme
poverty nor again
excessive wealth, for
both are productive
of great evil.

No matter how
hard you fight the
darkness, every light
casts a shadow, and
the closer you get to
the light, the darker
that shadow becomes.

Love is a madness
produced by an
unsatisfiable rational
desire to understand
the ultimate truth
about the world.

All men are by nature equal, made all of the same earth by one Workman; and however we deceive ourselves, as dear unto God is the poor peasant as the mighty prince.

The people have always some champion whom they set over them and nurse into greatness.... This and no other is the root from which a tyrant springs; when he first appears he is a protector.

Only a philosopher's mind grows wings, since its memory always keeps it as close as possible to those realities by being close to which the gods are divine.

Let him know how to
choose the mean and
avoid the extremes
on either side, as
far as possible....
For this is the way
of happiness.

Meno: I feel, somehow, that I like what you are saying.

Socrates: And I, Meno, like what I am saying. Some things I have said of which I am not altogether confident. But that we shall be better and braver and less helpless if we think that we ought to inquire, than we should have been if we indulged in the idle fancy that there was no knowing and no use in seeking to know what we do not know; — that is a theme upon which I am ready to fight, in word and deed, to the utmost of my power.

You are young, my son,
and, as the years go by,
time will change and
even reverse many of
your present opinions.
Refrain therefore
awhile from setting
yourself up as a judge
of the highest matters.

If the study of all these sciences which we have enumerated, should ever bring us to their mutual association and relationship, and teach us the nature of the ties which bind them together, I believe that the diligent treatment of them will forward the objects which we have in view, and that the labor, which otherwise would be fruitless, will be well bestowed.

There is in every one
of us, even those who
seem to be most
moderate, a type
of desire that is
terrible, wild,
and lawless.

Come then, and let us
pass a leisure hour
in storytelling, and
our story shall be
the education of
our heroes.

So where it is a general rule that it is wrong to gratify lovers, this can be attributed to the defects of those who make that rule: the government's lust for rule and the subjects' cowardice.

For this feeling of
wonder shows that you
are a philosopher,
since wonder is the
only beginning of
philosophy.

Oh dear Pan and all the other Gods of this place, grant that I may be beautiful inside. Let all my external possessions be in friendly harmony with what is within. May I consider the wise man rich. As for gold, let me have as much as a moderate man could bear and carry with him.

Welcome out of the cave, my friend. It's a bit colder out here, but the stars are just beautiful.

It is the task of the enlightened not only to ascend to learning and to see the good but to be willing to descend again to those prisoners and to share their troubles and their honors, whether they are worth having or not. And this they must do, even with the prospect of death.

Either we shall
find what it is we
are seeking or at
least we shall free
ourselves from the
persuasion that we
know what we do
not know.

The affairs of music
ought, somehow, to
terminate in the
love of the
beautiful.

Your silence
gives consent.

The true champion of justice, if he intends to survive even for a short time, must necessarily confine himself to private life and leave politics alone.

As a breeze or an echo
rebounds from the
smooth rocks and
returns whence it
came, so does the
stream of beauty,
passing through the
eyes which are the
windows of the soul,
come back to the
beautiful one.

He who has not contemplated the mind of nature which is said to exist in the stars, and gone through the previous training, and seen the connection of music with these things, and harmonized them all with laws and institutions, is not able to give a reason of such things as have a reason.

The poets are nothing
but interpreters of
the gods, each one
possessed by the
divinity to whom
he is in bondage.

Knowledge is the food of the soul; and we must take care, my friend, that the Sophist does not deceive us when he praises what he sells, like the dealers wholesale or retail who sell the food of the body; for they praise indiscriminately all their goods, without knowing what are really beneficial or hurtful.

And whenever any one informs us that he has found a man who knows all the arts, and all things else that anybody knows, and every single thing with a higher degree of accuracy than any other man -whoever tells us this, I think that we can only imagine him to be a simple creature who is likely to have been deceived by some wizard or actor whom he met, and whom he thought all-knowing, because he himself was unable to analyze the nature of knowledge and ignorance and imitation.

Excess of liberty,
whether it lies in
state or individuals,
seems only to pass
into excess of
slavery.

At the touch of
love everyone
becomes a poet.

The madness
of love is the
greatest of
heaven's
blessings.

Made in the USA
Las Vegas, NV
03 December 2024

13313879R10065